This journal belongs to

_____Linda_____

Happy moments – Praise God
Difficult moments – Seek God
Quiet moments – Worship God
Painful moments – Trust God
Every moment – Thank God.

You are a beloved child of God,
precious to Him in every way.
As you seek Him each new day,
He will show you the mysteries of life
and unfold His unique plans for you—
a life full of rich blessing.

God's love for you is new every morning.
He cares about you and knows
all the desires of your heart.
Let this journal inspire you to express your thoughts,
record your prayers, embrace your dreams,
and rejoice in God's daily blessings.

Be strong in the Lord, and may you experience
His new life every morning.

New Every Morning

With God, life is eternal—both in quality and length.
There is no joy comparable to the joy of discovering
something new from God, about God. If the continuing life
is a life of joy, we will go on discovering, learning.

EUGENIA PRICE

Take on an entirely new way of life—
a God-fashioned life, a life renewed from the inside
and working itself into your conduct
as God accurately reproduces his character in you.

EPHESIANS 4:24 MSG

Each dawn holds a new hope for a new plan,
making the start of each day the start of a new life.

GINA BLAIR

In the morning let our hearts gaze upon God's love
and the love He has allowed us to share,
and in the beauty of that vision,
let us go forth to meet the day.

ROY LESSIN

That is God's call to us—simply to be people
who are content to live close to Him and to renew
the kind of life in which the closeness
is felt and experienced.

THOMAS MERTON

That loneliness consumes some people in the group. That is so sad to me. People have to force themselves to be in community with others.

Picture of God's Love.
Unconditional Love
Sacrificial Love
Comforting Love
Quiet Love

F orgetting
A
I
Trust
Him

He has given me a new song to sing,
a hymn of praise to our God.
Many will see what he has done and be amazed.
They will put their trust in the Lord.

PSALM 40:3–4 NLT

A Heart Full of Praise

Let us give all that lies within us...to pure praise,
to pure loving adoration, and to worship from a grateful
heart—a heart that is trained to look up.

AMY CARMICHAEL

May you be filled with joy, always thanking the Father.
He has enabled you to share in the inheritance
that belongs to his people, who live in the light.
For he has rescued us from the kingdom of darkness
and transferred us into the Kingdom of his dear Son.

COLOSSIANS 1:11–13 NLT

Let's praise His name! He is holy, He is almighty.
He is love. He brings hope, forgiveness, heart cleansing,
peace, and power. He is our deliverer and coming King.
Praise His wonderful name!

LUCILLE M. LAW

The thought of You stirs us so deeply
that we cannot be content unless we praise You,
because You have made us for Yourself
and our hearts find no peace until they rest in You.

AUGUSTINE

John
1) – 18)   BFS
              Bible Study
                 Fellowship

Intro of Jesus
1-18 (1:9 - 4:54)

Jesus Ministry as God's Son
Chapters 5 – 10

Crisis in Jerusalem
11 – 12

Jesus w/ Disciples
13 – 17

Trial, Death & Burial
18 & 19

Resurrection & Conclusion
20 – 21

Life Light

The caterpillar must yield up the life it knows
and submit to the mystery of interior transformation.
It emerges from the process transfigured, with wings
that give it freedom to fly.... A rule of life gives us
a way to enter into the lifelong process
of personal transformation. Its disciplines help us
to shed the familiar but constricting "old self"
and allow our "new self" in Christ to be formed—
the true self that is naturally attracted to the light of God.

MARJORIE THOMPSON

The kiss of eternal life, and the warm embrace
of God's Word, are so sweet, and bring such pleasure,
that you can never become bored with them;
you always want more.

HILDEGARD OF BINGEN

In the beginning was the Word, and the Word
was with God, and the Word was God.
He was with God in the beginning.
Through him all things were made; without him
nothing was made that has been made. In him was life,
and that life was the light of all mankind.

JOHN 1:1–4 NIV

*W*e best glorify Him when His life
is seen through us as a light to others.

Always There

When we are told that God, who is our dwelling place,
is also our fortress, it can only mean one thing, and that is,
that if we will but live in our dwelling place,
we shall be perfectly safe and secure from every assault
of every possible enemy that can attack us.

HANNAH WHITALL SMITH

What a beautiful home, God...!
I've always longed to live in a place like this,
Always dreamed of a room in your house,
where I could sing for joy to God-alive!...
And how blessed all those in whom you live,
whose lives become roads you travel;
They wind through lonesome valleys, come upon brooks,
discover cool springs and pools brimming with rain!
God-traveled, these roads curve up the mountain,
and at the last turn—Zion! God in full view!

PSALM 84:1-2, 5-7 MSG

God is always present in the temple of your heart—
His home. And when you come in to meet Him there,
you find that it is the one place of deep satisfaction
where every longing is met.

*A*lways be in a state of expectancy,
and see that you leave room for God
to come in as He likes.

OSWALD CHAMBERS

The Music of God

From the heart of God comes the strongest rhythm—
the rhythm of love. Without His love reverberating in us,
whatever we do will come across like a noisy gong
or a clanging symbol. And so the work of the human heart,
it seems to me, is to listen for that music
and pick up on its rhythms.

KEN GIRE

He speaks, and the sound of His voice
is so sweet the birds hush their singing.
And the melody that He gave to me
within my heart is ringing.
And He walks with me, and He talks with me,
and He tells me I am His own.
And the joy we share as we tarry there
none other has ever known.

C. AUSTIN MILES

Let God have you, and let God love you—
and don't be surprised if your heart begins
to hear music you've never heard and your feet
learn to dance as never before.

MAX LUCADO

*S*ing songs to the tune of his glory,
set glory to the rhythms of his praise.

PSALM 66:2 MSG

Grace and Gratitude

Grace and gratitude belong together like heaven and earth.
Grace evokes gratitude like the voice an echo.
Gratitude follows grace as thunder follows lightning.

KARL BARTH

Life itself, every bit of health that we enjoy,
every hour of liberty and free enjoyment,
the ability to see, to hear, to speak, to think,
and to imagine—all this comes from the hand of God.
We show our gratitude by giving back to Him
a part of that which He has given to us.

BILLY GRAHAM

Praise the LORD!
For he has heard my cry for mercy.
The LORD is my strength and shield.
I trust him with all my heart.
He helps me, and my heart is filled with joy.
I burst out in songs of thanksgiving.

PSALM 28:6–7 NLT

Gratitude consists in a watchful, minute attention
to the particulars of our state, and to the multitude
of God's gifts, taken one by one. It fills us
with a consciousness that God loves and cares for us,
even to the least event and smallest need of life.

HENRY EDWARD MANNING

I will bless the LORD at all times;
His praise shall continually be in my mouth.

PSALM 34:1 NASB

Special Plans

This is the real gift: you have been given
the breath of life, designed with a unique,
one-of-a-kind soul that exists forever—
the way that you choose to live it
doesn't change the fact that you've been given
the gift of being now and forever.
Priceless in value, you are handcrafted by God,
who has a personal design and plan for each of us.

WENDY MOORE

All the days ordained for me
were written in your book
before one of them came to be.

PSALM 139:16 NIV

Allow your dreams a place in your prayers and plans.
God-given dreams can help you move
into the future He is preparing for you.

Remember you are very special to God
as His precious child. He has promised to complete
the good work He has begun in you.
As you continue to grow in Him,
He will teach you to be a blessing to others.

GARY SMALLEY AND JOHN TRENT

The LORD will work out his plans for my life—
for your faithful love, O LORD, endures forever.

PSALM 138:8 NLT

Glorious Handiwork

You are a creation of God unequaled
anywhere in the universe.
God never made anyone else exactly like you,
and He never will again. Thank Him for yourself
and then for all the rest of His glorious handiwork.

NORMAN VINCENT PEALE

The huge dome of the sky is of all things
sensuously perceived the most like infinity.
When God made space and worlds that move in space,
and clothed our world with air, and gave us such eyes
and such imaginations as those we have,
He knew what the sky would mean to us....
We cannot be certain that this was not indeed
one of the chief purposes for which Nature was created.

C. S. LEWIS

Wherever we look in the realm of nature,
we see evidence for God's design and exquisite care
for His creatures. Whether we examine the cosmos
on its largest scale or its tiniest, His handiwork is evident....
God's fingerprints are visible.

HUGH ROSS

> *You are worthy, our Lord and God, to receive glory and honor and power, for you created all things.*
>
> REVELATION 4:11 NIV

Made for Joy

Our hearts were made for joy. Our hearts were made
to enjoy the One who created them. Too deeply planted
to be much affected by the ups and downs of life,
this joy is a knowing and a being known by our Creator.
He sets our hearts alight with radiant joy.

These things I have spoken to you, that my joy
may be in you, and that your joy may be full.

JOHN 15:11 ESV

If one is joyful, it means that one is faithfully living
for God, and that nothing else counts;
and if one gives joy to others, one is doing God's work.
With joy without and joy within, all is well.

JANET ERSKINE STUART

Joyful are those who have the God of Israel as their helper,
whose hope is in the LORD their God.

PSALM 146:5 NLT

Live for today but hold your hands open to tomorrow.
Anticipate the future and its changes with joy.
There is a seed of God's love in every event,
every circumstance, every unpleasant situation
in which you may find yourself.

BARBARA JOHNSON

The joy of the Lord is your strength.

Nehemiah 8:10 nkjv

Wonder and Praise

Worship is [our] response to God's revelation of Himself.
It is expressing wonder, awe, and gratitude
for the worthiness, the greatness, and the goodness
of our Lord. It is the appropriate response
to God's person, His provision,
His power, His promises, and His plan.

NANCY LEIGH DEMOSS

Clap your hands, all you nations;
shout to God with cries of joy.
For the LORD Most High is awesome,
the great King over all the earth!...
Sing praises to God, sing praises;
sing praises to our King, sing praises.
For God is the King of all the earth;
sing to him a psalm of praise.

PSALM 47:1–2, 6–7 NIV

Like supernatural effervescence,
praise will sometimes bubble up from the joy
of simply knowing Christ. Praise like that is...
delight. Pure pleasure!

JONI EARECKSON TADA

The love of the Father is like a sudden rain shower
that will pour forth when you least expect it,
catching you up into wonder and praise.

Richard J. Foster

God Is Great

The simple fact of being…in the presence of the Lord
and of showing Him all that I think, feel, sense,
and experience, without trying to hide anything,
must please Him. Somehow, somewhere, I know
that He loves me, even though I do not feel that love
as I can feel a human embrace, even though
I do not hear a voice as I hear human words
of consolation…. God is greater than my senses,
greater than my thoughts, greater than my heart.
I do believe that He touches me in places
that are unknown even to myself.

HENRI J. M. NOUWEN

Have you ever thought what a wonderful privilege it is
that every one each day and each hour of the day
has the liberty of asking God
to meet him in the inner chamber
and to hear what He has to say?

ANDREW MURRAY

How abundant are the good things
that you have stored up for those who fear you,
that you bestow in the sight of all,
on those who take refuge in you.

PSALM 31:19 NIV

God is the sunshine that warms us,
the rain that melts the frost and waters the young plants.
The presence of God is a climate of strong
and bracing love, always there.

JOAN ARNOLD

The Source

He is the Source. Of everything. Strength for your day.
Wisdom for your task. Comfort for your soul.
Grace for your battle. Provision for each need.
Understanding for each failure.
Assistance for every encounter.

JACK HAYFORD

We are forgiven and righteous because of Christ's sacrifice;
therefore we are pleasing to God in spite of our failures.
Christ alone is the source of our forgiveness,
freedom, joy, and purpose.

ROBERT S. MCGEE

We must drink deeply from the very Source
the deep calm and peace of interior quietude
and refreshment of God, allowing the pure water
of divine grace to flow plentifully
and unceasingly from the Source itself.

MOTHER TERESA

You are never alone.
In your heart of hearts, in the place where
no two people are ever alike, Christ is waiting for you.
And what you never dared hope for springs to life.

BROTHER ROGER OF TAIZÉ

*For from Him and through Him
and to Him are all things.
To Him be the glory forever.*

ROMANS 11:36 NASB

Celebrate Today

One who loves is borne on wings;
he runs, and is filled with joy; he is free and unrestricted.
He gives all to receive all, and he has all in all;
for beyond all things he rests in the one highest thing,
from whom streams all that is good.

THOMAS À KEMPIS

Through all eternity to You a joyful song I'll raise;
for oh! eternity's too short to utter all Your praise.

JOSEPH ADDISON

Rejoice! Celebrate all the good things that GOD,
your God, has given you and your family.

DEUTERONOMY 26:10–11 MSG

If we are cheerful and contented, all nature smiles…
the flowers are more fragrant, the birds sing more sweetly,
and the sun, moon, and stars all appear more beautiful,
and seem to rejoice with us.

ORISON SWETT MARDEN

Live realistically. Give generously.
Adapt willingly. Trust fearlessly. Rejoice daily.

CHARLES SWINDOLL

Oh give thanks to the Lord.... Glory in his holy name;
let the hearts of those who seek the Lord rejoice!

1 Chronicles 16:8–10 esv

Heart and Soul

The "air" which our souls need also envelops
all of us at all times and on all sides.
God is round about us in Christ on every hand,
with many-sided and all-sufficient grace.
All we need to do is to open our hearts.

OLE HALLESBY

Deep within us all there is an amazing inner sanctuary
of the soul, a holy place...to which we may
continuously return. Eternity is at our hearts,
pressing upon our time-torn lives, warming us...
calling us home unto Itself. Yielding to these persuasions...
utterly and completely, to the Light within,
is the beginning of true life.

THOMAS R. KELLY

Grant me, Lord, to spread true love in the world.
Grant that by me and by your children it may penetrate
a little into all circles, all societies.... Grant that it may
penetrate the hearts of men and that I may never forget
that the battle for a better world is a battle of love,
in the service of love.

MICHAEL QUOIST

My heart, O God, is steadfast;
I will sing and make music with all my soul.

PSALM 108:1 NIV

Praise for This Day

Does not all nature around me praise God?
If I were silent, I should be an exception to the universe.
Does not the thunder praise Him as it rolls like drums
in the march of the God of armies? Do not the mountains
praise Him when the woods upon their summits wave
in adoration? Does not the lightning write His name
in letters of fire? Has not the whole earth a voice?
And shall I, can I, silent be?

CHARLES H. SPURGEON

For you make me glad by your deeds, LORD;
I sing for joy at what your hands have done.
how profound your thoughts!

PSALM 92:4–5 NIV

O God, great and wonderful, who has created the heavens,
dwelling in the light and beauty of it...
teach me to praise You, even as the lark
which offers her song at daybreak.

ISIDORE OF SEVILLE

Then your light will break forth like the dawn,
and your healing will quickly appear;
then your righteousness will go before you,
and the glory of the LORD will be your rear guard.

ISAIAH 58:8 NIV

*W*hen morning gilds the skies,
My heart awakening cries:
May Jesus Christ be praised!

JOSEPH BARNBY

Knowing Him More

This life is not all. It is an "unfinished symphony"...
with those who know that they are related to God
and have felt the power of an endless life.

HENRY WARD BEECHER

Consider Jesus. Know Jesus. Learn what kind of Person
it is you say you trust and love and worship.
Soak in the shadow of Jesus. Saturate your soul
with the ways of Jesus. Watch Him.
Listen to Him. Stand in awe of Him.
Let Him overwhelm you with the way He is.

JOHN PIPER

Joy comes from knowing God loves me
and knows who I am and where I'm going...
that my future is secure as I rest in Him.

DR. JAMES DOBSON

Know that the LORD is God.
It is he who made us, and we are his;
We are his people, the sheep of his pasture.

PSALM 100:3 NIV

God knows the rhythm of my spirit
and knows my heart thoughts.
He is as close as breathing.

So let us know, let us press on to know the LORD....
He will come to us like the rain,
like the spring rain watering the earth.

HOSEA 6:3 NASB

Fresh Hope

God...rekindles burned-out lives with fresh hope,
restoring dignity and respect to their lives—
a place in the sun! For the very structures
of earth are GOD's; he has laid out his operations
on a firm foundation.

1 SAMUEL 2:7–8 MSG

For what you have done I will always praise you
in the presence of your faithful people.
And I will hope in your name, for your name is good.

PSALM 52:9 NIV

The hope we have in Christ is an absolute certainty.
We can be sure that the place Christ is preparing for us
will be ready when we arrive, because with Him nothing
is left to chance. Everything He promised He will deliver.

BILLY GRAHAM

So our hope is in the LORD.
He is our help, our shield to protect us.
We rejoice in him,
because we trust his holy name.
LORD, show your love to us
as we put our hope in you.

PSALM 33:20–22 NCV

Though seen through many a tear,
Let not my star of hope grow dim or disappear.

BENJAMIN SCHMOLCK

A River of Delights

Your love, O Lord, reaches to the heavens,
your faithfulness to the skies.
Your righteousness is like the highest mountains,
your justice like the great deep....
How priceless is your unfailing love, O God!
People take refuge in the shadow of your wings.
They feast on the abundance of your house;
you give them drink from your river of delights.
For with you is the fountain of life;
in your light we see light.

PSALM 36:5–9 NIV

God's love is like a river springing up
in the Divine Substance and flowing endlessly
through His creation, filling all things
with life and goodness and strength.

THOMAS MERTON

Behold, I will do a new thing,
Now it shall spring forth;
Shall you not know it?
I will even make a road in the wilderness
And rivers in the desert.

ISAIAH 43:19 NKJV

A pure spirit is a sparkling stream, full of clear thought, and continually renewed in the crystal river of God's love.

JANET L. SMITH

There Every Day

I look behind me and you're there,
then up ahead and you're there, too—
your reassuring presence, coming and going.
This is too much, too wonderful—
I can't take it all in!

PSALM 139:5–6 MSG

I believe that God is in me as the sun is in the color
and fragrance of a flower—the Light in my darkness,
the Voice in my silence.

HELEN KELLER

Where can I go from your Spirit?
Where can I flee from your presence?
If I go up to the heavens, you are there;
if I make my bed in the depths, you are there.
If I rise on the wings of the dawn,
if I settle on the far side of the sea,
even there your hand will guide me,
your right hand will hold me fast.

PSALM 139:7–10 NIV

Know by the light of faith that God is present,
and be content with directing all your actions toward Him.

BROTHER LAWRENCE

I am with you and will watch over you wherever you go.

GENESIS 28:15 NIV

Praises Ring

Dear Lord,...shine through me,
and be so in me that every soul I come in contact
with may feel Your presence in my soul....
Let me thus praise You in the way You love best,
by shining on those around me.

JOHN HENRY NEWMAN

O LORD, you are my God; I will exalt you;
I will praise your name, for you have done wonderful
things, plans formed of old, faithful and sure.

ISAIAH 25:1 ESV

If you have never heard the mountains singing,
or seen the trees of the field clapping their hands,
do not think because of that they don't.
Ask God to open your ears so you may hear it,
and your eyes so you may see it, because,
though few people ever know it,
they do, my friend, they do.

MCCANDLISH PHILLIPS

Praise God from whom all blessings flow;
Praise Him, all creatures here below;
Praise Him above, ye heav'nly host:
Praise Father, Son, and Holy Ghost.

KEN THOMAS

You have turned my mourning into joyful dancing...
that I might sing praises to you and not be silent.
O Lord my God, I will give you thanks forever!

Psalm 30:11–12 nlt

Gifts to Cherish

Everything in life is most fundamentally a gift.
And you receive it best, and you live it best,
by holding it with very open hands.

LEO O'DONOVAN

Make the least of all that goes
and the most of all that comes.
Don't regret what is past. Cherish what you have.
Look forward to all that is to come.
And most important of all,
rely moment by moment on Jesus Christ.

GIGI GRAHAM TCHIVIDJIAN

People should eat and drink and enjoy the fruits
of their labor, for these are gifts from God.

ECCLESIASTES 3:13 NLT

Time is a very precious gift of God;
so precious that it's only given to us moment by moment.

AMELIA BARR

Your life is a gift from God,
And it is a privilege to share it.
Today and always,
Know that you have a
Very special place in others' hearts—
And in His.

The free gift of God is eternal life
through Christ Jesus our Lord.

ROMANS 6:23 NLT

God Wants You

Listening to God is a firsthand experience....
God invites *you* to vacation in His splendor.
He invites *you* to feel the touch of His hand.
He invites *you* to feast at His table.
He wants to spend time with *you*.

MAX LUCADO

The Most High calls to us and waits for us to respond.
He desires to quench our deepest thirst,
to satisfy our deepest hunger, and to fill us
with His power and presence as we dwell
in the secret place of the Most High.

CYNTHIA HEALD

Jesus declared, "I am the bread of life.
Whoever comes to me will never go hungry,
and whoever believes in me will never be thirsty."

JOHN 6:35 NIV

He is a God who can be found. A God who can be known.
A God who wants to be close to us. That's why
He is called Immanuel, which means "God with us."
But He draws close to us as we draw close to Him.

STORMIE OMARTIAN

*God is always speaking to us. Listen to Him.
He wants from us deep love, compassion, and forgiveness.*

MOTHER TERESA

Reflections of God

Just as a prism of glass miters light and casts a colored
braid, a garden sings sweet incantations the human heart
strains to hear. Hiding in every flower, in every leaf,
in every twig and bough, are reflections of the God
who once walked with us in Eden.

The heavens proclaim the glory of God.
The skies display his craftsmanship.
Day after day they continue to speak;
night after night they make him known.
They speak without a sound or word;
their voice is never heard.
Yet their message has gone throughout the earth,
and their words to all the world.

PSALM 19:1–4 NLT

Whether we are poets or parents or teachers or artists
or gardeners, we must start where we are
and use what we have. In the process of creation
and relationship, what seems mundane and trivial may
show itself to be holy, precious, part of a pattern.

LUCI SHAW

All the different things we desire are really one;
for they are reflections of aspects of God.

PETER KREEFT

I Will Rejoice

I know the Lord is always with me.
I will not be shaken, for he is right beside me.
No wonder my heart is glad, and I rejoice.
My body rests in safety....
You will show me the way of life,
granting me the joy of your presence
and the pleasures of living with you forever.

Psalm 16:8–9, 11 nlt

A joyful spirit is like a sunny day;
it sheds a brightness over everything;
it sweetens our circumstances and soothes our souls.

I will greatly rejoice in the Lord;
my soul shall exult in my God,
for he has clothed me with the garments of salvation;
he has covered me with the robe of righteousness.

Isaiah 61:10 esv

Even when we cannot see the why and wherefore
of God's dealings, we know that there is love
in and behind them, and so we can rejoice always.

J. I. Packer

The godly will rejoice in the Lord and find shelter in him.
And those who do what is right will praise him.

Psalm 64:10 nlt

Let the heavens rejoice, let the earth be glad;
let them say among the nations, "The Lord reigns!"

1 Chronicles 16:31 niv

The Light Inside

We are His only witnesses. God is counting on each of us.
No angel has been given the job. We are the lanterns—
Christ is the light inside.

OLETA SPRAY

My love of You, O Lord, is not some vague feeling:
it is positive and certain. Your word struck into my heart
and from that moment I loved You. Besides this,
all about me, heaven and earth and all that they contain
proclaim that I should love You.

AUGUSTINE

God's children who joyously know and claim
who they are and whose they are,
will be most likely to manifest the family likeness,
just because they know they are His children.

ALICE CHAPIN

When God has become our shepherd, our refuge,
our fortress, then we can reach out to Him in the midst
of a broken world and feel at home while still on the way.

HENRI J. M. NOUWEN

*S*ing to the Lord, praise his name;
proclaim his salvation day after day.

Psalm 96:2 niv

The Lord Bless You

The LORD bless you and keep you;
The LORD make His face shine upon you,
And be gracious to you;
The LORD lift up His countenance upon you,
And give you peace.

NUMBERS 6:24–26 NKJV

Drink freely of God's power and experience
His touch of refreshment and blessing.

ANABEL GILLHAM

May the favor of the Lord our God rest upon us;
establish the work of our hands for us—
yes, establish the work of our hands.

PSALM 90:17 NIV

Thank God that even when we are not worthy
of His blessings, He still loves us
and bestows peace, joy, and happiness.

GARY SMALLEY AND JOHN TRENT

Have you ever thought that in every action
of grace in your heart you have the whole omnipotence
of God engaged to bless you?

ANDREW MURRAY

God bless you and utterly satisfy your heart…
with Himself.

AMY CARMICHAEL

Redeemed

Praise the LORD, O my soul,
and forget not all his benefits—
who forgives all your sins and heals all your diseases,
who redeems your life from the pit
and crowns you with love and compassion,
who satisfies your desires with good things
so that your youth is renewed like the eagle's.

PSALM 103:2–5 NIV

When we focus on God, the scene changes.
He's in control of our lives; nothing lies outside the realm
of His redemptive grace. Even when we make mistakes,
fail in relationships, or deliberately make bad choices,
God can redeem us.

PENELOPE J. STOKES

Jesus is the Savior, but He is even more than that!
He is more than a Forgiver of our sins. He is even more
than our Provider of eternal life. He is our Redeemer!
He is the One who is ready to recover and restore
what the power of sin and death has taken from us.

JACK HAYFORD

But the Lord will redeem those who serve him.
No one who takes refuge in him will be condemned.

Psalm 34:22 nlt

Delight in the Lord

Dear Lord, grant me the grace of wonder.
Surprise me, amaze me, awe me in every crevice
of your universe. Delight me to see how your Christ plays
in ten thousand places… to the Father through
the features of men's faces. Each day enrapture me
with your marvelous things without number.
I do not ask to see the reason for it all;
I ask only to share the wonder of it all.

ABRAHAM JOSHUA HESCHEL

In almost everything that touches
our everyday life on earth, God is pleased
when we're pleased. He wills that we be as free as birds
to soar and sing our maker's praise without anxiety.

A. W. TOZER

Take delight in the LORD
and he will give you the desires of your heart.
Commit your way to the LORD;
trust in him and he will do this:
He will make your righteousness shine like the dawn,
your vindication like the noonday sun.

PSALM 37:4–6 NIV

Just slipping quietly into the presence of God
can be so exotic and fresh that it delights us enormously.

RICHARD J. FOSTER

Then my soul will rejoice in the LORD
and delight in his salvation.

PSALM 35:9 NIV

Extravagance of Soul

In extravagance of soul we seek His face.
In generosity of heart, we glean His gentle touch.
In excessiveness of spirit, we love Him
and His love comes back to us a hundredfold.

Tricia McCary Rhodes

We cannot kindle when we will
The fire that in the heart resides
The spirit bloweth and is still
In mystery our soul abides.

Matthew Arnold

God's holy beauty comes near you, like a spiritual scent,
and it stirs your drowsing soul.... He creates in you
the desire to find Him and run after Him—
to follow wherever He leads you, and to press peacefully
against His heart wherever He is.

John of the Cross

Love is extravagant in the price it is willing to pay,
the time it is willing to give, the hardships it is willing
to endure, and the strength it is willing to spend.
Love never thinks in terms of "how little,"
but always in terms of "how much."
Love gives, love knows, and love lasts.

Joni Eareckson Tada

Trust steadily in God, hope unswervingly,
love extravagantly.
And the best of the three is love.

1 CORINTHIANS 13:13 MSG

Give Thanks

It is right and good that we, for all things, at all times,
and in all places, give thanks and praise to You, O God.
We worship You, we confess to You, we praise You,
we bless You, we sing to You, and we give thanks to You:
Maker, Nourisher, Guardian, Healer,
Lord, and Father of all.

LANCELOT ANDREWES

True prayer is synonymous with gratitude
and contentment.... How marvelous prayer
is for communicating our delight with God.

GLORIA GAITHER

There is an activity of the spirit, silent, unseen,
which must be the dynamic of any form of truly creative,
fruitful trust. When we commit a predicament,
a possibility, a person to God in genuine confidence,
we do not merely step aside and tap our foot
until God comes through. We remain involved.
We remain in contact with God in gratitude and praise.

EUGENIA PRICE

You are my God, and I will praise you;
you are my God, and I will exalt you.
Give thanks to the LORD, for he is good;
his love endures forever.

PSALM 118:28–29 NIV

*G*ive thanks to the Lord and proclaim his greatness.
Let the whole world know what he has done.

1 Chronicles 16:8 nlt

Completely Loved

The grace of God means something like: Here is your life.
You might never have been, but you *are* because
the party wouldn't have been complete without you.
Here is the world. Beautiful and terrible things
will happen. Don't be afraid. I am with you.
Nothing can ever separate us.
It's for you I created the universe. I love you.

FREDERICK BUECHNER

We have come to know and to believe the love
that God has for us. God is love, and whoever abides
in love abides in God, and God abides in him.

1 JOHN 4:16 ESV

I will rejoice in doing them good,
and I will plant them in this land in faithfulness,
with all my heart and all my soul.

JEREMIAH 32:41 ESV

The heart is rich when it is content,
and it is always content when its desires are fixed on God.
Nothing can bring greater happiness
than doing God's will for the love of God.

MIGUEL FEBRES CORDERO-MUÑOZ

What good news! God knows me completely
and still loves me.

We love Him because He first loved us.

1 John 4:19 NKJV

Glory on Display

God is here! I hear His voice
While thrushes make the woods rejoice.
I touch His robe each time I place
My hand against a pansy's face.
I breathe His breath if I but pass
Verbenas trailing through the grass.
God is here! From every tree
His leafy fingers beckon me.

MADELEINE AARON

By reading of Scripture I am so renewed that all nature
seems renewed around me and with me.
The sky seems to be a purer, a cooler blue,
the trees a deeper green, light is sharper on the outlines
of the forest and the hills and the whole world
is charged with the glory of God.

THOMAS MERTON

LORD, everything you have made will praise you;
those who belong to you will bless you.
They will tell about the glory of your kingdom
and will speak about your power.
Then everyone will know the mighty things you do.

PSALM 145:10–12 NCV

> *Yours, O Lord, is the greatness and the power and the glory and the majesty and the splendor, for everything in heaven and earth is yours.*
>
> 1 Chronicles 29:11 niv

Blessing on Blessing

God is a rich and bountiful Father,
and He does not forget His children,
nor withhold from them anything
which it would be to their advantage to receive.

J. K. MACLEAN

You're blessed when you're content
with just who you are—no more, no less.
That's the moment you find yourselves proud owners
of everything that can't be bought.

MATTHEW 5:5 MSG

If anyone would tell you the shortest, surest way
to happiness and all perfection, he must tell you
to make it a rule to yourself to thank and praise God
for everything that happens to you.
For it is certain that whatever…happens to you,
if you thank and praise God for it,
you turn it into a blessing.

WILLIAM LAW

God, who is love—who is, if I may say it this way,
made out of love—simply cannot help
but shed blessing on blessing upon us.

HANNAH WHITALL SMITH

*I will send down showers in season;
there will be showers of blessing.*

EZEKIEL 34:26 NIV

Living Joy

Joy cannot be pursued. It comes from within.
It is a state of being. It does not depend on circumstances,
but triumphs over circumstances. It produces a gentleness
of spirit and a magnetic personality.

BILLY GRAHAM

For the Kingdom of God is not a matter
of what we eat or drink, but of living a life of goodness
and peace and joy in the Holy Spirit.

ROMANS 14:17 NLT

How necessary it is to cultivate a spirit of joy....
To act lovingly is to begin to feel loving, and certainly
to act joyfully brings joy to others which in turn
makes one feel joyful. I believe we are called
to the duty of delight.

DOROTHY DAY

Where does constant joy abound?
In the restless social round,
Entertainment in excess,
Worldly charm or cleverness?
Fleeting are their seeming gains.
Joy is found where Jesus reigns.

HALLIE SMITH BIXBY

*T*hough you have not seen him, you love him.
Though you do not now see him, you believe in him
and rejoice with joy that is inexpressible.

1 PETER 1:8 ESV

Enfolded in Peace

I will let God's peace infuse every part of today.
As the chaos swirls and life's demands pull at me
on all sides, I will breathe in God's peace that surpasses
all understanding. He has promised that He would set
within me a peace too deeply planted to be affected
by unexpected or exhausting demands.

WENDY MOORE

Calm me, O Lord, as You stilled the storm,
Still me, O Lord, keep me from harm.
Let all the tumult within me cease,
Enfold me, Lord, in Your peace.

CELTIC TRADITIONAL

Nothing in all creation is so like God as stillness.

MEISTER ECKHART

Instead of worrying, pray.
Let petitions and praises shape your worries
into prayers, letting God know your concerns.
Before you know it, a sense of God's wholeness,
everything coming together for good, will come
and settle you down. It's wonderful what happens when
Christ displaces worry at the center of your life.

PHILIPPIANS 4:6–7 MSG

I am leaving you with a gift—
peace of mind and heart.

JOHN 14:27 NLT

New Life

For God is, indeed, a wonderful Father who longs
to pour out His mercy upon us, and whose majesty
is so great that He can transform us from deep within.

TERESA OF ÁVILA

To pray is to change. This is a great grace.
How good of God to provide a path whereby our lives
can be taken over by love and joy and peace
and patience and kindness and goodness and faithfulness
and gentleness and self-control.

RICHARD J. FOSTER

Even though on the outside it often looks like things
are falling apart on us, on the inside, where God is making
new life, not a day goes by without his unfolding grace.

2 CORINTHIANS 4:16 MSG

Life begins each morning....
Each morning is the open door to a new world—
new vistas, new aims, new tryings.

LEIGH MITCHELL HODGES

Create in me a clean heart, O God;
and renew a steadfast spirit within me.

PSALM 51:10 NKJV

*G*od puts each fresh morning, each new chance of life, into our hands as a gift to see what we will do with it.

Full of Wonder

We need to recapture the power of imagination;
we shall find that life can be full of wonder,
mystery, beauty, and joy.

SIR HAROLD SPENCER JONES

When I need a dose of wonder I wait for a clear night
and go look for the stars.... In the country the great river
of the Milky Way streams across the sky, and I know
that our planet is a small part of that river of stars....
Often the wonder of the stars is enough
to return me to God's loving grace.

MADELEINE L'ENGLE

May our lives be illumined
by the steady radiance
renewed daily,
of a wonder,
the source of which
is beyond reason.

DAG HAMMARSKJÖLD

All heaven will praise your great wonders, LORD;
myriads of angels will praise you for your faithfulness.
For who in all of heaven can compare with the LORD?

PSALM 89:5–6 NLT

Show the wonders of your great love....
Keep me as the apple of your eye;
hide me in the shadow of your wings.

PSALM 17:7–8 NIV

Rich in Kindness

All praise to God, the Father of our Lord Jesus Christ,
who has blessed us with every spiritual blessing
in the heavenly realms because we are united with Christ.
Even before he made the world, God loved us and chose us
in Christ to be holy and without fault in his eyes.
God decided in advance to adopt us into his own family
by bringing us to himself through Jesus Christ.
This is what he wanted to do, and it gave him
great pleasure. So we praise God for the glorious grace
he has poured out on us who belong to his dear Son.
He is so rich in kindness and grace that he purchased
our freedom with the blood of his Son and forgave our sins.
He has showered his kindness on us,
along with all wisdom and understanding.

EPHESIANS 1:3–8 NLT

The LORD appeared to us…saying:
"I have loved you with an everlasting love;
I have drawn you with unfailing kindness."

JEREMIAH 31:3 NIV

GOD is all mercy and grace—
not quick to anger, is rich in love.

PSALM 145:8 MSG

Herein is grace and graciousness!
Herein is love and loving kindness! How it opens to us
the compassion of Jesus—so gentle, tender, considerate!

CHARLES H. SPURGEON

Take Time

It may seem strange to think that God wants to spend time
with us, but...think about it. If God went to all the trouble
to come to earth, to live the life that He did, to die for us,
then there's got to be a hunger and a passion behind that.
We think of prayer as an "ought to," but in reality
it is a response to God's passionate love for us.
We need to refocus on the fact that God is waiting
for us to show up and be with Him
and that our presence truly touches Him.

Dr. Henry Cloud

Come and sit and ask Him whatever is on your heart.
No question is too small, no riddle too simple.
He has all the time in the world.
Come and seek the will of God.

Max Lucado

Intimacy may not be rushed....
We can't dash into God's presence
and choke down spiritual inwardness
before we hurry to our one o'clock appointment.
Inwardness is time-consuming,
open only to minds willing to sample spirituality
in small bites, savoring each one.

Calvin Miller

*I've loved you the way my Father has loved me.
Make yourselves at home in my love.*

JOHN 15:9 MSG

God Is Good

All we are and all we have is by the...love of God!
The goodness of God is infinitely more wonderful
than we will ever be able to comprehend.

A. W. TOZER

Open your mouth and taste, open your eyes and see—
how good GOD is. Blessed are you who run to him.
Worship GOD if you want the best;
worship opens doors to all his goodness.

PSALM 34:8–9 MSG

The Lord's goodness surrounds us at every moment.
I walk through it almost with difficulty,
as through thick grass and flowers.

R. W. BARBER

All that is good, all that is true, all that is beautiful...
be it great or small, be it perfect or fragmentary,
natural as well as supernatural,
moral as well as material, comes from God.

JOHN HENRY NEWMAN

We walk without fear, full of hope
and courage and strength to do His will,
waiting for the endless good which He is always giving
as fast as He can get us able to take it in.

GEORGE MACDONALD

I remain confident of this: I will see the goodness
of the LORD in the land of the living.

PSALM 27:13 NIV

A Meaningful Life

When we allow God the privilege of shaping our lives,
we discover new depths of purpose and meaning.
What a joyful thought to realize you
are a chosen vessel for God perfectly suited for His use.

JONI EARECKSON TADA

What we feel, think, and do this moment influences
both our present and the future in ways
we may never know. Begin. Start right where you are.
Consider your possibilities and find inspiration…
to add more meaning and zest to your life.

ALEXANDRA STODDARD

I believe that nothing that happens to me is meaningless,
and that it is good for us all that it should be so,
even if it runs counter to our own wishes. As I see it,
I'm here for some purpose, and I only hope I may fulfill it.
In the light of the great purpose
all our privations and disappointments are trivial.

DIETRICH BONHOEFFER

The meaning of earthly existence lies,
not as we have grown used to thinking, in prospering,
but in the development of the soul.

ALEXANDER SOLZHENITSYN

It's in Christ that we find out who we are
and what we are living for.
Long before we first heard of Christ...he had his eye on us,
had designs on us for glorious living.

EPHESIANS 1:11–12 MSG

Prayers for Today

Be still, and in the quiet moments,
listen to the voice of your heavenly Father.
His words can renew your spirit....
No one knows you and your needs like He does.

JANET L. SMITH

Lord...give me the gift of faith to be renewed
and shared with others each day.
Teach me to live this moment only,
looking neither to the past with regret,
nor the future with apprehension.
Let love be my aim and my life a prayer.

ROSEANN ALEXANDER-ISHAM

Lord, make me an instrument of Your peace.
Where there is hate, may I bring love;
Where offense, may I bring pardon;
May I bring union in place of discord;
Truth replacing error;
Faith, where once there was doubt;
Hope, for despair;
Light, where once there was darkness;
Joy to replace sadness.

FRANCIS OF ASSISI

*T*oday, Lord, bless this place and time
that I've set aside to be with You.
And bless all those I pray for.

PATRICIA LORENZ

For Himself

The reason for loving God is God Himself,
and the measure in which we should love Him
is to love Him without measure.

BERNARD OF CLAIRVAUX

Although it be good to think upon the kindness of God,
and to love Him and worship Him for it; yet it is far better
to gaze upon the pure essence of Him and to love Him
and worship Him for Himself.

We desire many things, and God offers us only one thing.
He *can* offer us only one thing—Himself.
He has nothing else to give. There *is* nothing else to give.

PETER KREEFT

Observe how Christ loved us.
His love was not cautious but extravagant.
He didn't love in order to get something from us
but to give everything of himself to us.

EPHESIANS 5:1–2 MSG

There is an essential connection between
experiencing God, loving God, and trusting God.
You will trust God only as much as you love Him,
and you will love Him to the extent
you have touched Him, rather that He has touched you.

BRENNAN MANNING

I live by faith in the Son of God,
who loved me and gave himself for me.

GALATIANS 2:20 NIV

Grace Never Fails

God has not promised skies always blue,
flower-strewn pathways all our lives through;
God has not promised sun without rain,
joy without sorrow, peace without pain.
But God has promised strength for the day,
rest for the labor, light for the way,
grace for the trials, help from above,
unfailing sympathy, undying love.

ANNIE JOHNSON FLINT

God is adequate as our keeper....
Your faith will not fail while God sustains it;
you are not strong enough to fall away
while God is resolved to hold you.

J. I. PACKER

Keep a firm grip on the faith.
The suffering won't last forever. It won't be long before
this generous God who has great plans for us in Christ—
eternal and glorious plans they are!—
will have you put together and on your feet for good.

1 PETER 5:10–11 MSG

Grace...like the Lord, the Giver,
never fails from age to age.

JOHN NEWTON

From his abundance we have all received one gracious blessing after another.

JOHN 1:16 NLT

My Father's World

When I look at the galaxies on a clear night—
when I look at the incredible brilliance of creation,
and think that this is what God is like,
then instead of feeling intimidated and diminished by it,
I am enlarged—I rejoice that I am part of it.

MADELEINE L'ENGLE

This is my Father's world;
He shines in all that's fair.
In the rustling grass I hear Him pass;
He speaks to me everywhere.

MALTBIE D. BABCOCK

How beautiful it is to be alive!
To wake each morn as if the Maker's grace
Did us afresh from nothingness derive.
That we might sing "How happy is our case!
How beautiful it is to be alive."

HENRY SEPTIMUS SUTTON

Above all give me grace to use these beauties of earth
without me and this eager stirring of life within me
as a means whereby my soul may rise from creature
to Creator, and from nature to nature's God.

JOHN BAILLIE

The earth is the LORD's, and all its fullness,
The world and those who dwell therein.

PSALM 24:1 NKJV

The Light of His Glory

The Son radiates God's own glory and expresses
the very character of God, and he sustains
everything by the mighty power of his command.
When he had cleansed us from our sins,
he sat down in the place of honor at the right hand
of the majestic God in heaven.

HEBREWS 1:3 NLT

In heaven our light will be provided by an infallible source,
the Son of God. And nothing will interfere
with our basking in His fellowship.

MARILYN M. MORGAN

God also has highly exalted Him and given Him the name
which is above every name, that at the name of Jesus
every knee should bow, of those in heaven,
and of those on earth, and of those under the earth,
and that every tongue should confess
that Jesus Christ is Lord, to the glory of God the Father.

PHILIPPIANS 2:9–11 NKJV

The Word became human and made his home among us.
He was full of unfailing love and faithfulness.
And we have seen his glory,
the glory of the Father's one and only Son.

JOHN 1:14 NLT

Turn your eyes upon Jesus, look full
in His wonderful face, and the things of earth will grow
strangely dim, in the light of His glory and grace.

HELEN H. LEMMEL

Sacred Moments

We are always in the presence of God....
There is never a non-sacred moment!
His presence never diminishes.
Our awareness of His presence may falter,
but the reality of His presence never changes.

MAX LUCADO

Whom have I in heaven but You?
And besides You, I desire nothing on earth.
My flesh and my heart may fail, but God is the strength
of my heart and my portion forever....
As for me, the nearness of God is my good;
I have made the Lord GOD my refuge.

PSALM 73:25–26, 28 NASB

The ability to see and the practice of seeing God
and God's world comes through a process of seeking
and growing in intimacy with Him.

DALLAS WILLARD

If each moment is sacred—a time and place
where we encounter God—life itself is sacred.

JEAN M. BLOMQUIST

> *The reflective life is a way of living that heightens our spiritual senses to all that is sacred.*
>
> KEN GIRE

Our Faithful Father

Lift up your eyes. Your heavenly Father waits to bless you—
in inconceivable ways to make your life
what you never dreamed it could be.

ANNE ORTLUND

Just as a father has compassion on his children,
So the LORD has compassion on those who fear Him.
For He Himself knows our frame;
He is mindful that we are but dust....
But the lovingkindness of the LORD
is from everlasting to everlasting
on those who fear Him,
And His righteousness to children's children.

PSALM 103:13–14, 17 NASB

God takes care of His own....
At just the right moment
He steps in and proves Himself
as our faithful heavenly Father.

CHARLES SWINDOLL

My child, don't reject the LORD's discipline,
and don't be upset when he corrects you.
For the LORD corrects those he loves,
just as a father corrects a child in whom he delights.

PROVERBS 3:11–12 NLT

I will sing of the mercies of the LORD forever;
With my mouth will I make known
Your faithfulness to all generations.

PSALM 89:1 NKJV

The Most Beautiful Things

The beauty of the earth, the beauty of the sky,
the order of the stars, the sun, the moon...
their very loveliness is their confession of God,
for who made these lovely mutable things,
but He who is Himself unchangeable beauty?

AUGUSTINE

As God's workmanship, we deserve to be treated,
and to treat ourselves, with affection and affirmation,
regardless of our appearance or performance.

MARY ANN MAYO

Your beauty should come from within you—
the beauty of a gentle and quiet spirit
that will never be destroyed and is very precious to God.

1 PETER 3:4 NCV

You are God's created beauty
and the focus of His affection and delight.

JANET L. SMITH

In all ranks of life the human heart yearns
for the beautiful, and the beautiful things
that God makes are His gift to all alike.

HARRIET BEECHER STOWE

The best and most beautiful things
in the world cannot be seen or even touched.
They must be felt with the heart.

HELEN KELLER

New Light

Into all our lives, in many simple, familiar...ways,
God infuses this element of joy from the surprises of life,
which unexpectedly brighten our days,
and fill our eyes with light.

SAMUEL LONGFELLOW

Brightness of my Father's glory,
Sunshine of my Father's face,
Let Your glory ever shine on me,
Fill me with Your grace.

JEAN SOPHIA PIGOTT

It doesn't take a huge spotlight to draw attention
to how great our God is. All it takes is for one committed
person to so let His light shine before men,
that a world lost in darkness welcomes the light.

GARY SMALLEY AND JOHN TRENT

The day is done, the sun has set,
Yet light still tints the sky;
My heart stands still
In reverence,
For God is passing by.

RUTH ALLA WAGER

*Every good and perfect gift is from above,
coming down from the Father of the heavenly lights.*

JAMES 1:17 NIV

Our Fulfillment

In comparison with this big world,
the human heart is only a small thing.
Though the world is so large, it is utterly unable
to satisfy this tiny heart. Our ever growing soul
and its capacities can be satisfied only in the infinite God.
As water is restless until it reaches its level,
so the soul has no peace until it rests in God.

Sadhu Sundar Singh

You have set Your glory above the heavens.
Thy glory flames from sun and star:
Center and soul of every sphere,
Yet to each loving heart how near.

Oliver Wendell Holmes

So faith bounds forward to its goal in God,
and love can trust her Lord to lead her there;
upheld by Him my soul is following hard,
till God hath full fulfilled my deepest prayer.

Frederick Brook

We are never more fulfilled than when
our longing for God is met by His presence in our lives.

Billy Graham

He is Lord of heaven and earth....
He himself gives life and breath to everything,
and he satisfies every need.

Acts 17:24–25 NLT

Praise for the Promises

Commit to hope. There's reason to! For the believer,
hope is divinely assured things that aren't here yet!
Our hope is grounded in unshakable promises.

JACK HAYFORD

The fulfillment of God's promise depends entirely
on trusting God and his way, and then simply embracing
him and what he does. God's promise arrives as pure gift.

ROMANS 4:16 MSG

Faith, in the Old Testament, is defined by a person's
willingness to wait for the promises of God to come.
Faith, in the New Testament,
means following the Promised One.

MICHAEL CARD

Our thanksgiving today should include those things
which we take for granted, and we should continually
praise our God, who is true to His promise, who has
provided and retained the necessities for our living.

BETTY FUHRMAN

We may…depend upon God's promises, for…
He will be as good as His word.
He is so kind that He cannot deceive us,
so true that He cannot break His promise.

MATTHEW HENRY

Jesus Christ opens wide the doors of the treasure house
of God's promises, and bids us go in and take
with boldness the riches that are ours.

CORRIE TEN BOOM

Joy Is...

Joy is the touch of God's finger.
The object of our longing is not the touch
but the Toucher. This is true of all good things—
they are all God's touch. Whatever we desire,
we are really desiring God.

PETER KREEFT

Joy is really a road sign pointing us to God.
Once we have found God...we no longer need
to trouble ourselves so much about the quest for joy.

C. S. LEWIS

Ask, using my name, and you will receive,
and you will have abundant joy.

JOHN 16:24 NLT

Joy is more than my spontaneous expression of laughter,
gaiety, and lightness. It is deeper than an emotional
expression of happiness. Joy is a growing, evolving
manifestation of God in my life as I walk with Him.

BONNIE MONSON

I pray that God, the source of hope, will fill you
completely with joy and peace because you trust in him.
Then you will overflow with confident hope through
the power of the Holy Spirit.

ROMANS 15:13 NLT

Joy is the echo of God's life within us.

Enduring Faithfulness

Praise the LORD, all you nations.
Praise him, all you people of the earth.
For his unfailing love for us is powerful;
the LORD's faithfulness endures forever.

PSALM 117:1–2 NLT

Not merely does God will to guide us by showing us
His way;…whatever mistakes we may make,
we shall come safely home. Slippings and strayings
there will be, no doubt, but the everlasting arms
are beneath us; we shall be caught, rescued, restored.
This is God's promise; this is how good He is.
And our self-distrust, while keeping us humble,
must not cloud the joy with which we lean
on our faithful covenant God.

J. I. PACKER

You, O God, are both tender and kind,
not easily angered, immense in love,
and you never, never quit.

PSALM 86:15 MSG

God, who is faithful and just—and also full of mercy—
will forgive and *will* cleanse. Like the father
of the prodigal, He rushes to us at the first sign
of our turning toward home.

RICHARD J. FOSTER

Give thanks to the LORD, for he is good!
His faithful love endures forever.

PSALM 136:1 NLT

True Adoration

It's who you are and the way you live that count
before God. Your worship must engage your spirit
in the pursuit of truth. That's the kind of people
the Father is out looking for: those who are simply
and honestly *themselves* before him in their worship.
God is sheer being itself—Spirit. Those who worship
him must do it out of their very being, their spirits,
their true selves, in adoration.

JOHN 4:23–24 MSG

Prayer is a response to the outpouring love
and concern with which God lays siege to every soul.
When that reply to God is most direct of all,
it is called adoration. Adoration is loving back....
In adoration we enjoy God.
We ask nothing except to be near Him.

DOUGLAS V. STEERE

Sweet adoration, flows from your children;
Glory and honor and praise are a part
Of our constant devotion, love set in motion
For the Divine One, who reigns in our hearts.

BROWN BANNISTER, DAWN ROGERS,
AND LYNN SUTTER

*O*pen wide the windows of our spirits
and fill us full of light; open wide the door
of our hearts that we may receive and entertain Thee
with all the powers of our adoration.

CHRISTINA ROSSETTI

The Gift of Today

Experience God in the breathless wonder
and startling beauty that is all around you.
His sun shines warm upon your face. His wind whispers
in the treetops. Like the first rays of morning light,
celebrate the start of each day with God.

WENDY MOORE

Oh, how sweet the light of day,
And how wonderful to live in the sunshine!...
Don't take a single day for granted.
Take delight in each light-filled hour.

ECCLESIASTES 11:7–8 MSG

The sun...in its full glory, either at rising or setting—
this, and many other like blessings we enjoy daily;
and for the most of them, because they are so common,
most men forget to pay their praises. But let not us.

IZAAK WALTON

To be grateful is to recognize the Love of God
in everything He has given us—
and He has given us everything.
Every breath we draw is a gift of His love,
every moment of existence is a gift of grace.

THOMAS MERTON

*This is the day the LORD has made;
We will rejoice and be glad in it.*

PSALM 118:24 NKJV

Let Us Worship

When you open up the Bible and you pray the Scriptures
back to God, you're experiencing something
really wonderful....He's delighted.
The silence confirms that we are His people.
We are talking and God is listening.
But the best times are when God starts talking,
and we're quiet enough to hear Him.

CALVIN MILLER

If we begin to worship and come to God
again and again by meditating, by reading, by prayer,
and by obedience, little by little God becomes
known to us through experience.
We enter into a sweet familiarity with God,
and by tasting how sweet the Lord is we pass into...
loving God, not for our own sake, but for Himself.

BERNARD OF CLAIRVAUX

Come, let us worship and bow down,
let us kneel before the LORD our Maker.
For He is our God,
and we are the people of His pasture
and the sheep of His hand.

PSALM 95:6–7 NASB

*W*alk and talk and work and laugh with your friends.
But behind the scenes, keep up the life
of simple prayer and inward worship.

THOMAS KELLY

Echoes of Praise

By entering through faith into what God has always
wanted to do for us—set us right with him, make us fit
for him—we have it all together with God because
of our Master Jesus. And that's not all:
We throw open our doors to God and discover
at the same moment that he has already
thrown open his door to us. We find ourselves
standing where we always hoped we might stand—
out in the wide open spaces of God's grace and glory,
standing tall and shouting our praise.

ROMANS 5:1–2 MSG

For God, praise is the sweet echo
of His own excellence in the hearts of His people.
For us, praise is the summit of satisfaction
that comes from living in fellowship with God.

JOHN PIPER

Everything on earth will worship you;
they will sing your praises,
shouting your name in glorious songs.

PSALM 66:4 NLT

For all that I see that You do for me, I thank You.
For all that I do not see that You do for me, I praise You.

CHRISTOPHER DE VINCK

*S*hout to the Lord, all the earth;
break out in praise and sing for joy.

PSALM 98:4 NLT

Fullness of Life

I think what we're longing for is not "the good life"
as it's been advertised to us...but life in its fullness,
its richness, its abundance. Living more reflectively
helps us enter into that fullness.

KEN GIRE

To be used of God. Is there anything more encouraging,
more fulfilling? Perhaps not, but there is something
more basic: to meet with God. To linger in His presence,
to shut out the noise of the city and, in quietness,
give Him the praise He deserves.
Before we engage ourselves in His work,
let's meet Him in His Word...in prayer...in worship.

CHARLES SWINDOLL

You've always given me breathing room,
a place to get away from it all, a lifetime pass
to your safe-house, an open invitation as your guest.

PSALM 61:3 MSG

Our God is so wonderfully good, and lovely,
and blessed in every way that the mere fact of belonging
to Him is enough for an untellable fullness of joy!

HANNAH WHITALL SMITH

*L*ove wholeheartedly, be surprised,
give thanks and praise—then you will discover
the fullness of your life.

DAVID STEINDL-RAST

Pure Delight

The Lord's chief desire is to reveal Himself to you and,
in order for Him to do that, He gives you abundant grace.
The Lord gives you the experience of enjoying
His presence. He touches you, and His touch
is so delightful that, more than ever,
you are drawn inwardly to Him.

MADAME JEANNE GUYON

O the pure delight of a single hour
that before Thy throne I spend,
When I kneel in prayer, and with Thee, my God,
I commune as friend with friend!

FANNY CROSBY

Our Creator would never have made such lovely days,
and given us the deep hearts to enjoy them,
above and beyond all thought,
unless we were meant to be immortal.

NATHANIEL HAWTHORNE

The joyful birds prolong the strain,
their song with every spring renewed;
the air we breathe, and falling rain,
each softly whispers: God is good.

JOHN HAMPDEN GURNEY

All glory to God, who...will bring you with great joy
into his glorious presence.

JUDE 1:24 NLT

A Grateful Heart

Gratitude unlocks the fullness of life. It turns what we have
into enough, and more.... It can turn a meal into a feast,
a house into a home, a stranger into a friend.
Gratitude makes sense of our past, brings peace for today,
and creates a vision for tomorrow.

MELODY BEATTIE

Gratitude is the heart of contentment.
I have never met a truly thankful, appreciative person
who was not profoundly happy.

NEIL CLARK WARREN

Being grateful for what we have today
doesn't mean we have to have that forever.
It means we acknowledge that what we have today
is what we're supposed to have today.
There is enough.... And all we need will come to us.

Enter His gates with thanksgiving
And His courts with praise.
Give thanks to Him, bless His name.

PSALM 100:4 NASB

True gratitude, like true love,
must find expression in acts, not words.

R. MILDRED BARKER

*S*avor little glimpses of God's goodness and His majesty,
thankful for the gift of them.

A Sense of Wonder

Whether sixty or sixteen, there is in every
human being's heart the love of wonder,
the sweet amazement at the stars and starlike things,
the undaunted challenge of events,
the unfailing childlike appetite for what-next,
and the joy of…living.

SAMUEL ULLMAN

Many, O LORD my God,
are the wonders which You have done,
And Your thoughts toward us;
There is none to compare with You.
If I would declare and speak of them,
They would be too numerous to count.

PSALM 40:5 NASB

Isn't it a wonderful morning?
The world looks like something
God had just imagined for His own pleasure.

LUCY MAUD MONTGOMERY

All the world is an utterance of the Almighty.
Its countless beauties, its exquisite adaptations,
all speak to you of Him.

PHILLIPS BROOKS

*W*ho is like you—majestic in holiness,
awesome in glory, working wonders?

Exodus 15:11 NIV

Fully Satisfied

God is not only the answer to a thousand needs,
He is the answer to a thousand wants. He is the fulfillment
of our chief desire in all of life. For whether or not
we've ever recognized it, what we desire is unfailing love.
Oh, God, awake our souls to see—You are what we want,
not just what we need. Yes, our life's protection,
but also our heart's affection. Yes, our soul's salvation,
but also our heart's exhilaration. Unfailing love.
A love that will not let me go!

BETH MOORE

The LORD will guide you always;
he will satisfy your needs in a sun-scorched land....
You will be like a well-watered garden,
like a spring whose waters never fail.

ISAIAH 58:11 NIV

The God who created the vast resources of the universe
is also the inventor of the human mind.
His inspired words of encouragement guarantee us
that we can live above our circumstances.

DR. JAMES DOBSON

The greatest honor we can give God is to live gladly
because of the knowledge of His love.

JULIAN OF NORWICH

*S*atisfy us in the morning with your unfailing love,
that we may sing for joy and be glad all our days.

PSALM 90:14 NIV

A Day for Joy

A new day rose upon me. It was as if another sun
had risen into the sky; the heavens were indescribably
brighter, and the earth fairer; and that day has gone
on brightening to the present hour. I have known
the other joys of life.... I have known art and beauty,
music and gladness; I have known friendship
and love and family ties; but it is certain
that till we see GOD in the world—
GOD in the bright and boundless universe—
we never know the highest joy.

Orville Dewey

The miracle of joy is this:
It happens when there is no apparent reason for it.
Circumstances may call for despair.
Yet something different rouses itself inside us....
We are able to remember what the sunrise looks like....
We remember God. We remember He is love.
We remember He is near.

Ruth Senter

Those the LORD has rescued will return.
They will enter Zion with singing;
everlasting joy will crown their heads.
Gladness and joy will overtake them,
and sorrow and sighing will flee away.

Isaiah 35:10 NIV

Herein is joy, amid the ebb and flow
of the passing world: our God remains unmoved,
and His throne endures forever.

Robert E. Coleman

Jars of Clay

For God, who said, "Let there be light in the darkness,"
has made this light shine in our hearts so we could know
the glory of God that is seen in the face of Jesus Christ.
We now have this light shining in our hearts,
but we ourselves are like fragile clay jars
containing this great treasure. This makes it clear
that our great power is from God, not from ourselves.

2 CORINTHIANS 4:6–7 NLT

Recognizing who we are in Christ and aligning our life
with God's purpose for us gives a sense of destiny....
It gives form and direction to our life.

JEAN FLEMING

Troubles are often the tools by which God
fashions us for better things.

HENRY WARD BEECHER

When life becomes difficult, when cracks spread
through our existence and our strength seems to leak out,
fill the gaps with hope. Like gold adorning
distressed ancient art, hope will reinforce,
add value, and reveal more beauty.

BARBARA FARMER

Keep still, and He will mold you to the right shape.

MARTIN LUTHER

*L*ORD, you are our Father.
We are the clay, you are the potter;
we are all the work of your hand.

ISAIAH 64:8 NIV

Through His Creation

It is an extraordinary and beautiful thing that God,
in creation...works with the beauty of matter; the reality
of things; the discoveries of the senses, all five of them;
so that we, in turn, may hear the grass growing;
see a face springing to life in love and laughter....
The offerings of creation...our glimpses of truth.

MADELEINE L'ENGLE

I am convinced that God has built into all of us
an appreciation of beauty and has even allowed us
to participate in the creation of beautiful things and places.
It may be one way God brings healing to our brokenness,
and a way that we can contribute toward
bringing wholeness to our fallen world.

MARY JANE WORDEN

Lord Jesus Christ, You are the sun that always rises,
but never sets. You are the source of all life,
creating and sustaining every living thing....
May I walk in Your light, be nourished by Your food,
be sustained by Your mercy, and be warmed by Your love.

ERASMUS

Seeing how God works in nature
can help us understand how He works in our lives.

JANETTE OKE

Let the glory of the LORD endure forever;
Let the LORD be glad in His works.

PSALM 104:31 NASB

Fresh Morning

Bless You, O Lord, for the living arc of the sky
over me this morning. Bless You, O Lord,
for the companionship of night mist far above
the skyscraper peaks I saw when I woke
once during the night. Bless You, O Lord,
for the miracle of light to my eyes
and the mystery of it ever changing.

CARL SANDBURG

It is good to give thanks to the LORD
and to sing praises to Your name, O Most High;
to declare Your lovingkindness in the morning
and Your faithfulness by night.

PSALM 92:1–2 NASB

Old patterns are pinned to the fabric edges of my mind
this morning, Lord. Release the pins
with Your gentle fingers that my thoughts might flow
freely in new designs of Your shaping.

PHYLLIS VIERHELLER

His anger lasts only a moment, but his favor
lasts a lifetime; weeping may remain for a night,
but rejoicing comes in the morning.

PSALM 30:5 NIV

𝒮ee each morning a world made anew,
as if it were the morning of the very first day;...
treasure and use it, as if it were
the final hour of the very last day.

FAY HARTZEL ARNOLD

God Is Everywhere

There's not a tint that paints the rose
Or decks the lily fair,
Or marks the humblest flower that grows,
But God has placed it there....
There's not a place on earth's vast round,
In ocean's deep or air,
Where love and beauty are not found,
For God is everywhere.

You have...one God and Father of all, who rules over all,
works through all, and is present in all. Everything you are
and think and do is permeated with Oneness.

EPHESIANS 4:6 MSG

Lord, give me an open heart to find You everywhere,
to glimpse the heaven enfolded in a bud,
and to experience eternity in the smallest act of love.

MOTHER TERESA

Be strong and brave. Don't be afraid, because the LORD
your God will be with you everywhere you go.

JOSHUA 1:9 NCV

You already know that God is everywhere....
And where God is, there is heaven—*heaven!*
where His Majesty reigns in glory.

TERESA OF ÁVILA

My Presence shall go with you,
and I will give you rest.

Exodus 33:14 NASB

By Grace Alone

Grace tells us that we are accepted just as we are.
We may not be the kind of people we want to be,
we may be a long way from our goals, we may have
more failures than achievements, we may not be wealthy
or powerful or spiritual…but we are nonetheless
accepted by God, held in His hands.

McCullough

Grace binds you with far stronger cords than the cords
of duty or obligation can bind you. Grace is free,
but when once you take it, you are bound forever
to the Giver and bound to catch the spirit of the Giver.
Like produces like. Grace makes you gracious;
the Giver makes you give.

E. Stanley Jones

God is…the kind of God who freely acts
and passionately interacts with us in this world,
for in His own eternal Being He is the ever living,
loving, and acting God who will not be without us
but who in grace freely determines Himself
for us as our God and Savior.

Thomas Torrance

My grace is sufficient for you,
for my power is made perfect in weakness.

2 Corinthians 12:9 niv

The Highest Goal

Wisdom is the power to see, and the inclination to choose,
the best and highest goal, together with the surest means
of attaining it.... What makes life worthwhile is having
a big enough objective, something which catches
our imagination and lays hold of our allegiance....
What higher, more exalted, and more compelling goal
can there be than to know God?

J. I. PACKER

Lord Jesus Christ; Let me seek You by desiring You,
and let me desire You by seeking You;
let me find you by loving You,
and love You in finding You.

ANSELM OF CANTERBURY

Yes, LORD, walking in the way of your laws,
we wait for you; your name and renown
are the desire of our hearts.

ISAIAH 26:8 NIV

The more authentic our desires, the more they touch
upon our identities and also upon the reality of God
at the heart of our being. Our most authentic desires
spring ultimately from the deep inner wells
where the longing for God runs freely.

PHILIP SHELDRAKE

Great is Your love, higher than the heavens;
Your faithfulness reaches to the skies.
Be exalted, O God, above the heavens,
and let Your glory be over all the earth.

PSALM 108:3–5 NIV

Ellie Claire® Gift & Paper Expressions
Franklin, TN 37067
www.ellieclaire.com
Ellie Claire is a registered trademark of Worthy Media, Inc.

His Mercies Are New Every Morning Journal
© 2016 by Ellie Claire
Published by Ellie Claire, an imprint of Worthy Publishing Group,
a division of Worthy Media, Inc.

ISBN 978-1-63326-159-4

All rights reserved. No part of this book may be reproduced in any form except
for brief quotations in printed reviews, without permission in writing from the publisher.

The Holy Bible, King James Version (KJV). The Holy Bible, New International Version®, NIV® Copyright © 1973, 1978, 1984, 2011 by Biblica, Inc.® All rights reserved worldwide. The Holy Bible, New King James Version® (NKJV). Copyright © 1982 by Thomas Nelson, Inc. The Holy Bible, English Standard Version® (ESV®), copyright © 2001 by Crossway Bibles, a publishing ministry of Good News Publishers. The New American Standard Bible® (NASB), Copyright © 1960, 1962, 1963, 1968, 1971, 1972, 1973, 1975, 1977, 1995 by The Lockman Foundation. The Holy Bible, New Living Translation (NLT) copyright © 1996, 2004, 2007 by Tyndale House Foundation. Used by permission of Tyndale House Publishers Inc., Carol Stream, Illinois 60188. *The Message* (MSG). Copyright © 1993, 1994, 1995, 1996, 2000, 2001, 2002. Used by permission of NavPress Publishing Group. The New Century Version® (NCV). Copyright © 2005 by Thomas Nelson, Inc. Used by permission. All rights reserved.

Excluding Scripture verses and deity pronouns, in some quotations references to men and masculine pronouns have been replaced with gender-neutral or feminine references. Additionally, in some quotations we have carefully updated verb forms and wordings that may distract modern readers.

Stock or custom editions of Ellie Claire titles may be purchased in bulk for educational, business, ministry, fundraising, or sales promotional use.
For information, please e-mail info@EllieClaire.com

Compiled by Barbara Farmer
Cover by Melissa Reagan
Interior design by Bart Dawson

Printed in China.

1 2 3 4 5 6 7 8 9 RRD 21 20 19 18 17 16